For the hearts with missing pieces ~
They are here with us always,
watching from the stars.

Watching from the Stars

Written & illustrated
by Stacey McNeill

ISBN: 978-1-7396782-2-7

I know you can't be with me
But I still feel you near,
For little things keep happening
That show me you are here

Sometimes it's a special song
Or a penny on the ground,
Butterflies and clear night skies,
A feather floating down
A robin in the garden,
Sunflowers in a vase,
Signs that you are with me,
Watching from the stars

"I promise I'll never forget you,"
said the fox.

"We've shared too many happy times
to forget," replied the moon.

"I'll keep them in my heart forever,"
said the fox.

"That way we'll always be together,"
replied the moon.

The day your heart stopped beating
And we had to say goodbye,
One little star shone brighter
Than the others in the sky
So now amidst the darkness
When I need to feel your love,
I stare into the black of night
And look for you above

They say - in time - the pieces
Of my broken heart will heal,
But I'll never forget you
Or the way you made me feel
I know there are parts of me
That only you can mend,
So I'll keep them safe until the time
We're side by side again

"It feels so dark," said the fox,
"and darkness makes me feel so alone."

"The darkness can be lonely," replied the moon,
"but remember, you're never really alone in the
dark."

"What do you mean?"
asked the fox.

"The darkest nights
are when the stars shine
at their brightest,"
replied the moon,
"and do you know why?"

"Why?" asked the fox.

"Because they sparkle with all
the love from those we've lost,"
replied the moon, "so even in the
darkest times; there is hope, love
and light to be found."

One day I will be starlight
And you will still be here,
But even on the longest nights
I will still be near
So when you're left in darkness
And can't see your way through,
Remember there's a star above
Shining just for you

Why is it so difficult
To say that little word?
The loneliest and saddest one
I have ever heard
I know one day the time will come
When I will have to try,
But it will be the hardest thing
To have to say 'goodbye'

I didn't only lose you
At the time you passed away,
I've lost you many times since then
Almost every day
I lose you in the moments
We never got to share,
And every time I turn to you
To find that you're not there
I lose you in the sunsets
I know you'd love to see,
With every lonely autumn leaf
Clinging to a tree

I lose you in each falling tide
That sparkles 'neath the moon,
Each wave seeming to whisper
Memories of me and you
I lose you in the wonder
Of a midnight starry sky,
And every time I hear someone
Say the word 'goodbye'
I didn't only lose you
At the time you passed away,
I've lost you many times since then
Almost every day

"Why do goodbyes hurt so much?"
asked the fox.

"Because they remind us of how wonderful
something was," replied the moon," even if
we didn't realise it at the time."

"Are they forever?" asked the fox.

"Sometimes," replied the moon, "but so are
memories, and so in those moments you have
to stay strong, and remember the
amazing times you had."

If I could wish upon a star
I'd ask to touch the moon,
For up there in the sky is where
I could be with you
I wouldn't wish for fortune,
I wouldn't wish for fame,
I'd simply wish for one more day
To spend with you again

"Others want to see me be happy," said the fox, "but sometimes that feels like to much to manage... sometimes I just don't feel anything at all."

"You don't have to hide your pain, or feel ashamed of it," replied the moon, "grief is a journey, and it will take time for you to feel strong again."

"Will I ever feel whole?" asked the fox.

"You will find light in your life again," replied the moon, "you may never feel quite the same as before, but in time you will find your own, new kind of peace and happiness."

There's a precious piece of twine
Wrapped around my heart,
The other end is tied to yours
For when we are apart
The string cannot be broken
No matter near or far,
It'll reach right up into the sky
When you become a star

It was never meant to be this way
That we would be apart,
That instead of sitting next to me
You'd be only in my heart
I'm still navigating
How life looks on my own,
I didn't think I'd have to walk
Our path through life alone

I know you're there above me
Written in the stars,
And though we can't be together
You're forever in my heart
But in this sea of darkness
Alone but for the moon,
There aren't enough stars in the sky
To count the times I think of you

"I'll miss you when you've gone," said the fox.

"I know," replied the moon, "but I'll always be
with you in your heart."

"But I won't be able to see you," said the fox.

"You'll be able to feel me instead," replied the
moon, "each time you look up at the night sky
I'll be with you, sending love, hope and light."

"You'll be with the stars," said the fox.

"I will," smiled the moon.

I know it might feel like it, but
you are not alone.

I'm Stacey, and together with my husband, Jamie, I run a lovely little UK-based business called 'Fox Under The Moon', encouraging positivity and self love through words and pictures.
Welcome to our warm and whimsical world! x

Hello!

Jamie ↑

Me! ↗

← Pixie

I am passionate about the natural world, and as you'll see from my little illustrations; wildlife, woodlands and magical night skies inspire everything I create. My artwork is for all ages - it is inspired by the simplicity of everyday life, and the complicated emotions that go with it. I hope the little conversations between Fox, Moon and their friends can bring some encouragement and comfort to you and those you love.

For books, cards, prints and gifts, and for wholesale enquiries, please visit:

www.foxunderthemoon.co.uk